World Languages
for Kids
By Sachiko Otohata

Korean
English
Japanese
Italian
Persian
Spanish
Mandarin
German
French
Hindi
Swahili
Tagalog
Arabic
Russian
Portuguese

We have dedicated considerable time and effort to ensure the accuracy and cultural sensitivity of our content. However, if you find any errors or have suggestions, please feel free to contact us at factorysachi.com or via social media @factorysachi. Your input is crucial for us to refine and improve our offerings for young learners.

Copyright © 2023 Sachiko Otohata

All rights reserved. No part of this book may be used or reproduced in any manner whatsoever without written permission except in the case of brief quotations embodied in critical articles and reviews.

While the author has used their best efforts in preparing this book, they make no representations or warranties with respect to the accuracy or completeness of the content.

Writing and illustrations: **Sachiko Otohata**
Published in Canada

If you enjoyed this book, please consider leaving a review online. As an independent publisher, every review helps more parents and children discover and learn about this book.

🌐 factorysachi.com
📷 factorysachi (Instagram/Facebook/Pinterest)

Special thanks to all my international friends who generously helped me proofread this book. I'd also like to give a special thank you to my son, Ren, who always inspires me.

- Sachiko Otohata

My friends all have different backgrounds and speak different languages than I do.

It's exciting to learn how to say things their way!

Let's wander around and see what they say.

 English    Russian    French

 Tagalog   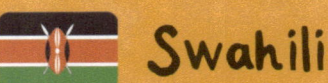 Swahili    Spanish

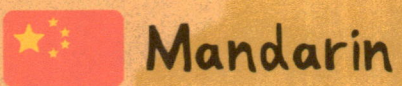 Mandarin   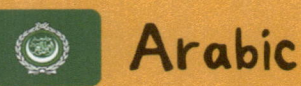 Arabic   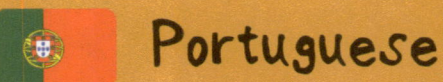 Portuguese

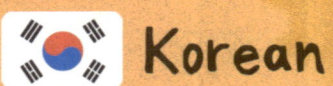 Korean   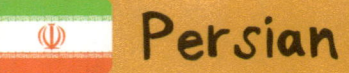 Persian   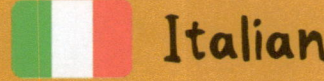 Italian

 Japanese    Hindi   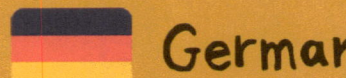 German

Pronunciation Guide:

How to write the word

(你好) **Nǐ hǎo**
Nee how

How to say the word

OR

Scan the QR code to hear the phrases!

www.factorysachi.com/qr/world-languages

 **Hola**
Oh-lah

Hallo
Hah-loh

Bonjour
Bohn-zhoor

Ciao
Chow

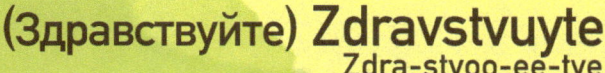 **(Здравствуйте) Zdravstvuyte**
Zdra-stvoo-ee-tye

Mambo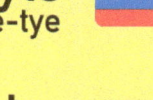
Mahm-boo

(مرحبا) Marhabaan
Mar-ha-baan

(سلام) Salâm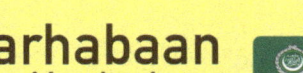
Sah-lahm

(नमस्ते) Namaste
Nah-mahs-tay

Kamusta
Kah-moo-stah

(你好) Nǐ hǎo
Nee how

(안녕하세요) Annyeonghaseyo
An-nyoung ha-seh-yo

(こんにちは) Konnichiwa
Kon-ni-chi-wa

(Спасибо) **Spasibo**
Spah-see-boh

Danke
Dahn-kuh

Gracias
Grah-see-ahs

Obrigado
Oh-bree-gah-doh

Grazie
Graht-see-eh

Asante
Ah-sahn-teh

(شكرا) **Shukraan**
Shoo-krahn

(ممنون) **Mamnūnam**
Mahm-noo-nahm

(धन्यवाद) **Dhanyavaad**
Dha-nya-vaad

Salamat
Sah-lah-maht

(谢谢) **Xièxiè**
Syeh-syeh

(고맙습니다) **Gomabseubnida**
Go-mahp-soob-nee-da

(ありがとう) **Arigatō**
Ah-ree-gah-toh

 **Mi dispiace**
Mee dee-spyah-cheh

Entschuldigung
Ent-shool-dee-goong

Je suis désolé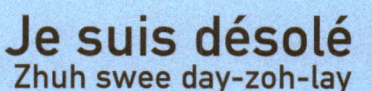
Zhuh swee day-zoh-lay

Lo siento
Loh syen-toh

Desculpe-me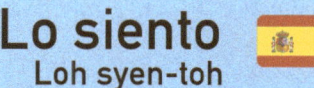
Dehs-kool-peh-meh

(Прости) **Prosti**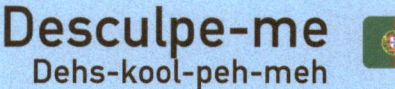
Pro-stee

Pole sana
Poh-leh sah-nah

(انا اسفة • انا اسف) **Ana asef • Ana asefah**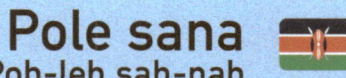
Ah-nah ah-sef • Ah-nah ah-se-foh

(متاسفم) **Motaassefam**
Moh-tah-se-fahm

(माफ़ करना) **Maaf karna**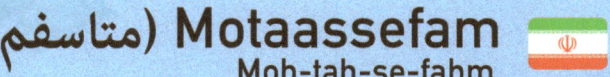
Mahf kar-nah

Paumanhin
Pah-oo-mahn-heen

(对不起) **Duìbuqǐ**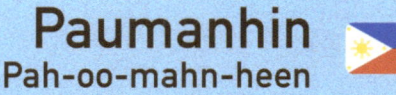
Dway-boo-chee

(죄송합니다) **Joesonghabnida**
Chway-song-hahb-nee-dah

Ich liebe dich
Ick lee-buh dik

Je t'aime
Zhuh tem

Te amo
Teh ah-moh

Eu te amo
Eh-oo cheh ah-moh

Ti amo
Tee ah-moh

(я люблю тебя) **Ya lyublyu tebya**
Yah lyoo-blyoo tee-byah

Ninakupenda
Nee-nah-koo-pen-dah

(أحبكِ • أحبكَ) **Uhibbuki • Uhibbuka**
Oo-hib-book-ee • Oo-hib-book-ah

(دوسِت دارم) **Dooset daram**
Doo-set dah-rahm

(मैं तुमसे प्यार करता हूँ) **Main tumase pyaar karta hoon**
Meh too-mah-say pyar kar-tah hoon

Mahal kita
Mah-hahl kee-tah

(我爱你) **Wǒ ài nǐ**
Woh eye nee

(사랑해) **Salang-hae**
Sah-lang-heh

(すきです) **Suki desu**
Soo-kee des

Now it's your turn!

Why don't we go out and make friends from all over the world...

Пойдем

On y va

...where many different people, languages, cultures, and especially YOU make it so unique and beautiful!

The End

World Languages for Kids Series

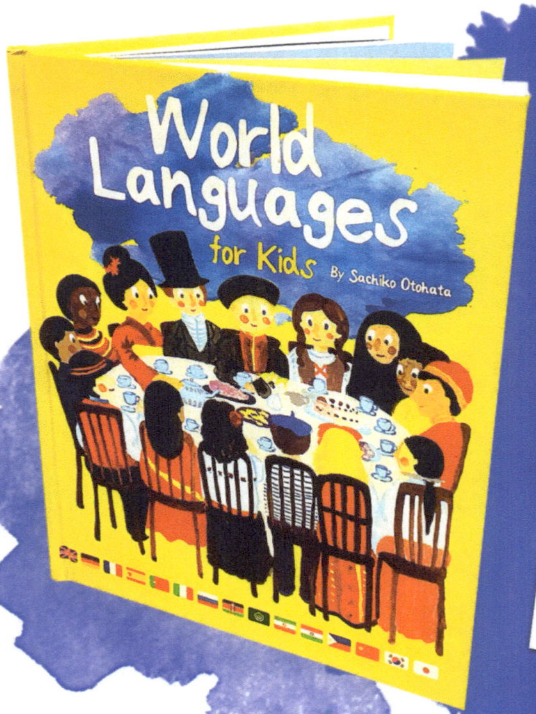

The series introduces ten common words in 15 languages.

English, German, Russian, French, Spanish, Portuguese, Italian, Persian, Arabic, Hindi, Tagalog, Swahili, Mandarin Chinese, Japanese, and Korean

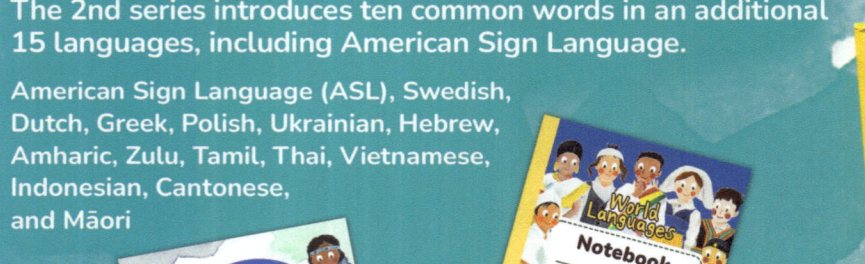

The 2nd series introduces ten common words in an additional 15 languages, including American Sign Language.

American Sign Language (ASL), Swedish, Dutch, Greek, Polish, Ukrainian, Hebrew, Amharic, Zulu, Tamil, Thai, Vietnamese, Indonesian, Cantonese, and Māori

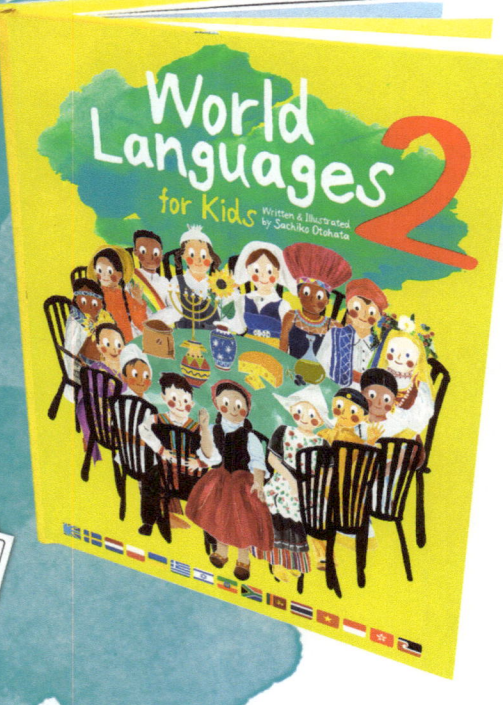

Follow us on:

 FactorySachi (Instagram/Facebook/Pinterest)

Please visit our website to view more products!
FactorySachi.com

www.ingramcontent.com/pod-product-compliance
Lightning Source LLC
Chambersburg PA
CBHW042249100526
44587CB00002B/77